I0163797

Kevin E Bowser

MOVING FROM VISION
TO
ACTION

§

*A practical guide for local churches to take
the all-important step of translating what they
believe into actionable, definable, and
measurable steps*

Leadership Voices, LLC
Humble, Texas

To my long-time friend, David Woods and to our co-conspirator for change, Bob Spalding. This book is a tribute to their work and their labor of love for Him and for His Kingdom.

For information about permission to reproduce selections from this book, write to Leadership Voices, LLC, 18611 Timber Twist Drive, Humble, Texas 77346

ISBN-13: 978-0692256053 (Leadership Voices, LLC)
ISBN-10: 0692256059

Creative and Formatting Attribution

Cover Art by bookDESIGN and purchased via
http://www.fiverr.com/bookdesign

Final formatting and layout by kindler and purchased via
http://www.fiverr.com/kindler

Printed in the United States of America

Table of Contents

Acknowledgments

I cannot imagine ever starting a project like this, much less finishing it and publishing it without the help of my friend, my Prayer Partner and my Brother in Christ, David Woods. Dave is a man of God and has dedicated his life to the service of the Lord. At the time that we worked on this project, Dave was an officer in the U.S. Air Force. He had a great and stable career in the military. But God had something else for him. Dave resigned his officer's commission and retired early from the Air Force. He now holds multiple degrees and academic credentials. Dave and his family now pastor in Virginia.

Robert Spalding, Special Agent for the F.B.I. was also very helpful and inspirational in developing this project. Bob was in many ways the "voice of reason" when two young bucks were out there seeking to change the world and reshape the way that local churches operate. Bob's calm and moderating personality helped us to achieve more than we ever could have achieved by ourselves. And we never forgot, he was carrying a gun!

My family was extremely supportive of my work during the time that this project was a living and current event. My kids had to make sacrifices sometimes as Dave and I met for many hours working on the restructuring and ministry enhancement at our local church. My wife had to endure probably the most as my head was so full of ideas and strategies that it nearly exploded at times. Many times she would be the sounding board late at night when no one else was around. She was and is the glue that holds my world together.

Abstract

This book is designed as a companion to a live workshop entitled, *"Moving from Vision to Action."* The *Moving from Vision to Action (MFV2A) methodology* has been used effectively in local churches to take the all-important steps to translate the vision that God has given them into real actionable steps. This all is part of the larger process of moving from vision-casting into more tactical processes to help the local church achieve its goals as stated in its core values and mission statement.

General overview

The workshop is both a look backward in review at what has worked in the past, but also it is a look forward in to the dynamic process of creating tangible and measurable steps to achieve the local church's goals. Following is a very simple outline of the key areas covered in the full workshop and that will be covered briefly in the pages of this book.

- As leaders, we must look at strategic planning principles and processes
- As leaders, we must revisit some areas of concern as noted in regular self-reviews, evaluations or surveys
- As leaders, we must go beyond our vision and into action
- As leaders, we must move into the all-important secondary and action phases of planning, and ultimately into a review of how well our actions are lining up with our vision and whether we are being successful

Setting

The workshop is designed to be conducted as an all-day event. It has proven to be most successful in an off-site setting that is designed for such purposes. Large hotels and conference centers make ideal settings. A few dollars spent to create a conducive and appropriate atmosphere will be well worth the expenditure. But smaller churches and organizations can achieve great results in an on-site meeting room or a Sunday School classroom converted for the day for such a purpose.

Morning Session

The morning session should be opened on a Spiritual note. It is largely a time of laying down some foundational principles that many of the leadership may not be exposed to on a regular basis. It closes with a time reviewing both lay and pastoral strengths and weaknesses. A time of food and fellowship bridges the morning and afternoon sessions and helps build and strengthen the bonds among the group. Below is a brief explanation of each session.

Prayer and Praise The workshop should begin with a focus on prayer and praise for all that God has done or is doing in the church. This time of worship will set the tone for all that will follow. It should be upbeat and inspirational. A companion tool is available from Leadership Voices, LLC that has some praise and worship choruses on easy to use PowerPoint presentations. These are ready for you to use and will need only minor modifications such as editing the master slide with your church's copyright license information.

Understanding the Successful Strategic Planning Process Many times we use words like "strategic planning" without a basic understanding of just what those terms mean. Many folks are accustomed to words like this in a secular or work environment. But they are not at all accustomed to hearing them in this type of setting. The subject of these terms and their applicability to a church or ministry setting is a topic for another book. However, this section lays the groundwork for much of the later discussion and action sections.

Review the Lay Leadership Self-Evaluation It is important to understand our current strengths and weaknesses as a prelude to building or expanding ministries. The end result of some of this review process may be that some long-standing ministries may no longer be an active part of the overall ministry of the church.

Review Pastoral Evaluation It is also important to understand and accept the strengths and weaknesses of the pastoral staff. Lay leadership must step up and lead in areas where their strengths offset pastoral weaknesses. However, if this process is to be successful, it must be done in an attitude of mutual respect and love between both laity and pastoral staff.

Afternoon Session

Following lunch, the workshop reconvenes and looks at some of the issues that came to light from the morning session. The bulk of the remaining time is spent in learning and, more importantly, applying the principles learned. Once again, a brief description of each follows.

Areas of Particular Significance Several key areas will surface from the evaluation review sections of the morning. This section will allow the participants to expand and respond to the prior evaluation review session.

Working the "Franklin Model" - Part 1 and Part 2 Using the Franklin Quest Model (now the Franklin

Covey model), the participants learn the valuable skills of determining their core values and developing a process to bring daily activities in line with those governing values.

A Time of Commitment It is important to close the day with a time of commitment to God, each other, and to the work of the church. This is as important to the overall success of the day as the opening worship time was in setting the tone of the day.

Challenges of the 21st Century

There are many challenges that face the church of the 21st century. The church is under attack and in many ways it is losing its relevance as an anchor of society. The purpose of this document is not to speak to the spiritual conditions of the church. Others are more qualified than I to do so. But rather, I am writing from the assumption that you as a church leader desire to strive for greatness. Not in a prideful way. But rather as a servant leader who is stepping out in faith as God calls each of us.

Below are brief examples of just some of these challenges that face the church today. They are included not as major discussion and debate items, but merely as empirical and statistical data.

- Church attendance is in decline
  - In 1971, 41% of the population would say they attended church
  - Today, only 37% would make the same claim
  - 46% of women attend church weekly
  - 26% of men attend weekly

- Most of the population is unclaimed for the Gospel
  - 2 / 3 of nearly any major metropolitan area population has no regular church home
  - No county in America is more "churched" today than it was 20 years ago

- Most church growth is transfer growth.

- 8 out of 10 "new members" are simply going from one church to another
- Mainstream and Denominational Churches are small and churches are closing.
  - In the US, 150 churches a week out of approximately 400,000 are closing
  - Others are being started, of course, but many are closing

- Mega-churches are gaining ground over the smaller and more intimate churches
  - Pervasive "seeker sensitivity" in the mega churches
  - Impact of Rick Warren and Joel Osteen on what a normal church looks like

- The groups we are ministering to are diverse
  - There is no longer a common understanding of the "Christian" language
  - We cannot assume a church background -- it most likely does not exist
  - Various sets of values in the different groups of our society make our task even harder

- Expectations are higher than ever
  - People know what they want out of a church
  - Pastoral leadership faces demanding lay leaders and congregations
  - Church facilities are to be state-of-the-art
  - Many times the performance is more important to folks than the message

- Commitment is lower than ever

- Active church persons are usually involved in no more than 2 activities a week, usually Sunday morning and 1 other
- The typical church goer misses 13 Sundays a year

● There are more distractions than ever
  - Everyone is going in at least 100 different directions.
  - Many things clamor for the attention of the believer

● The culture has a consumer mentality
  - "Church Shopping" is the norm these days
  - Assimilation becomes much more important, with only a 2-3 week window of opportunity
  - The average new convert is dropping out of the church within a couple of months because of lack of assimilation or lack of new friendships

● There is a lack of belief in absolutes
  - Three out of four believe there are no absolute truths
  - Even 70% of Christians do not acknowledge a set of absolute values by which they guide their lives, and this figure is higher as we get into the younger generations
  - We must challenge our young people to believe the fact that there are absolute truths in God's Word, and it never changes!

What will be the church's response?

How will you respond as a leader in your church? How will your church respond? What must the church do to be effective in the 21st century? These are fundamental leadership issues and questions that we are facing.

The specifics will be developed as the local church continues in this process. But, generally speaking, the following are true.

We must pray more than ever. We must become even more "a people of prayer." Prayer must permeate everything that the local church does.

We must be willing to evaluate more than ever. How and why are we doing what we are doing? Evaluation and analysis must become normal parts of the church board's regular activities.

We must be willing to plan more than ever. In the past "top down" planning and programs worked. But today we must be innovative and analytical of our plans. Pastors and lay leaders must work together to develop plans and activities together.

We must be willing to adapt more than ever. We should be planning for the people we are trying to reach, not for ourselves. We must not compromise values, but rather we must adapt our methods. The church must be able to manage change without losing its identity.

This book is necessary because of the leadership crisis that exists in the modern church. This is not meant to bash pastors or be taken overly negatively by the lay leadership. The fact of the matter is that pastors, elders and board members today did not create the environment in which we find ourselves. On the contrary, the environment and culture created them.

Likewise, this document is not intended to weigh in on the various views that various churches have on the role of deacon, elder, or board member. For our purposes let's agree that the laity have a role in leadership and that role is being defined and described differently depending on the local church context. Some see that role as active and providing direction and guidance to the church. Some see it more in terms of servant-leader and providing in reach and outreach to the congregation. Regardless of your view, the principles contained in the MFV2A process will work and will make your church more effective if you are willing to work the process.

One of the problems is that many pastors are not taught leadership skills in seminary. And they are only recently being taught any non-theological skills. The most successful pastoral leaders out there have developed these skills on their own or have sought to imitate those whom they view as having them and being worthy of imitation.

And let us not leave God out of the equation. It is God through the Holy Spirit that truly develops and empowers leaders for Kingdom work. But empowering by the Holy Spirit is not the focus of this author at this time. However, it is only by the power of the Holy Spirit that I am able to do anything worthy for Jesus Christ and His church.

Reaching Your Goals

General George Custer and the Battle of Little Big Horn

The following is a little piece of military history as recounted by Pastor David Woods of Melwood Church of the Nazarene. It is an excellent story to illustrate the importance of planning and execution in the eventual success (or failure) of a venture.

> *Gen. Custer's defeat was brought about by some very poor planning or in many ways, by no planning at all. The setting of this battle is at the very height of the Indian wars and took place in south central Montana. Gen. Custer was the Commander of the 7th Cavalry under Gen. Alfred Terry.*
>
> *Gen. Terry sent Custer north to be a blocking force as Terry's troops moved around to the north and then turned southward to fully surround the Indian encampment. This would trap the Indians between mountains on the east and west and between the two military forces to the north and south.*
>
> *A tragic series of events began when somewhat on a whim, Gen. Custer moved his forces an entire day early. He was confident that he could handle whatever resistance arose. He was unaware that he was about to encounter one of the largest Indian gatherings in the history of North America!*
>
> *Around noon, Custer divided his troops and sent 3 companies of men ahead to scout for Indians to the west. Two hours later, he sent 3 more companies to charge ahead into the Indian encampment that was the main objective.   He would gather the rest of his forces and*

attack from the east, over a ridge of mountains. He hastily sent a messenger rearward to call up his one remaining company of reserve troops.

As he approached from the east, the advancing troops hit an enormous wall of Indians advancing to the south to meet the approaching forces. The troops were nearly overrun. They immediately retreated and entrenched themselves in preparation for more fighting. Having also repulsed the initial attack from the south, the Indians turned their battle-frenzied attention toward Custer's units on the hillside to the east. Historians are not exact at this point, but indications are such that the Indian to Cavalry ratio was nearly 20 to 1 in favor of the Indians.

The battle lasted only a few hours and was sadly over before Gen. Terry's forces arrived to carry out his now destroyed plan. Custer and hundreds of soldiers were killed that day because of his impatience and utter lack of a sensible plan, not to mention his total disregard for the designated commanding general's plan.

If Gen. Custer had only stopped to analyze his situation and the objectives before him and adhered to the plan, he and his soldiers would have survived and avoided one of the worst military defeats in history. Instead he just jumped in as he thought best and became a personal victim in one of the worst battles in the history of United States military engagements.

A Historical Definition

Strategic planning origins are clearly military. The term itself has its genesis in ancient Greece. The literal meaning is "general of the army." *Strategoi* were generals of Greek tribal armies. These generals had impressive success on the Plains of Marathon nearly 2,500 years ago. These were elected political leaders. Although they left battlefield tactics to troop leaders, they ruled on policy issues as a group.

With that stated, let's examine our purpose as the leadership of the local church. The leadership of the church is to be the *strategoi*. And the ministry leadership board is composed of *strategoi* and exists to lead the local Church to impact the community for Christ.

Let's look at the key words in these early stages of reaching our goals and objectives.

Key Words
There are several key words that are helpful in understanding the importance of this matter of reaching our goals.

Impact - Impact upon the community and congregation is accomplished through the process of ministry.

Process - "Every work of literature begins with a single word, every journey a single step, every venture...one action."

A clear understanding and application of these principles would influence everything that we do. The key words would revise and clarify the statement below as follows.

Successful Process - Every Great work of Literature begins with a single *well chosen* word, every *triumphant* journey a single step *forward*, every *successful* venture....one *well planned* action."

The Two Types

There are two types of planning that I will consider for the purposes of this document. The first is Long-Term or Strategic Planning. And, by definition, it has a long-term perspective. As a result, it cannot be highly detailed and must deal with issues and subjects in broad terms. Details will be worked out in subsequent actions or processes.

The second is Short-Term or Tactical Planning. And that is really where this material is directed. As noted earlier, many churches are led by visionary leaders or have a sense of the grand picture of what God is calling them to do. However, they often lack the requisite skills to translate the big picture into smaller and more manageable sections. The old adage about eating an elephant is based partly upon tactical guidance. You eat that elephant one bite at a time. And short-term and tactical planning describes how to cut that elephant into bite-sized chunks.

Strategic or Long-Range Planning

A Vision for What God is Calling the Church to Do

A strategic or long-range plan usually has a 3-5 year horizon, duration, or lifespan, although 10 year strategic plans are not uncommon. In some industries 50 year plans are the norm. By day, I work for a major integrated energy company and we have 50 and 100 year plans to locate, reach and develop hydrocarbons that may currently be located in areas that are hostile environmentally, ecologically or geo-politically. We have to have a long-term view of the world to be successful.

So, do not be afraid of a 3 to 5 year plan. And have it reviewed and updated annually. It should be comprehensive to cover all ministries in the local church. This is not a detailed document. However, it is broad enough in its scope to encompass every major ministry of the church and have sufficient information about the ministries such that someone unfamiliar with that ministry could understand how it fits into the overall strategic plan of the church.

Strategic Planning Involves a Commitment from the Leadership

Leadership Commitment may be the most misunderstood portion of the overall process. Leadership in this instance is intended to encompass not only the pastor and staff, but also the elected lay leadership of the church. Also, it is critical that the non-elected leadership be included this process. Many leaders in the local church never have their name appear in nomination to serve in an elected capacity. John Maxwell popularized the phrase that *"leadership is influence"* and strategic planning had better involve the key influencers of the church or the chances of success drop precipitously.

Planning Horizon — Where does the local church need to be?

The planning horizon is part and parcel to the traditional vision-casting process. In this process the local church answers questions such as, "What would we be doing for Jesus Christ if money, facility and staff were not an issue?" Planning and vision-casting are not the times to put limits on God and think small. Think big and see what God can do through you with eyes of faith.

People Process — Involve entire congregation
Just as leadership commitment is important, so also is "followship commitment." There is an old Chinese proverb that says; *"He who thinks he is leading and has no one following... Is only taking a walk."* It is important to involve the entire congregation. It is important to "sell" the plan. Here again is an area where key influencers need to be considered and brought into the process. The more people who have ownership the greater the chances for success.

Systematic Elements —Analysis and evaluation
There is a systematic approach to long-range planning. It involves the logical analysis and evaluation of past, present and future ministries in the local church. In order to plan for the future we must first revisit the past and analyze the present. This is an oft-neglected process in the church. Every existing ministry or program of the church should be assessed or evaluated on at least an annual basis. Just like your financial records should be audited, so should your ministry results be audited and assessed.

Sequence and Timetable — "B" must follow "A"
The long-range planning process is very much a sequential and linear one. Many aspects of a long-range plan are highly dependent upon the successful completion of a prior step. Also, many steps are dependent upon completion by specific and predetermined dates. Much of our program runs

parallel to the academic calendar of the school system and in conjunction with the Christian calendar of holidays. It doesn't do anyone any good to plan a big Christmas musical production and not plan for that to align with the Advent season. Likewise, planning major youth events or retreats must coincide with the academic schedule if you expect to have anyone attend.

Recognized Barriers — Be sure we know the limits of our facility or resources

God's resources are infinite. That we can all agree upon. However, He moves and acts through the obedience and faithfulness of His people. That said, it is important to look realistically at the resources at hand. It is foolhardy to try to begin an elder care facility in an area where zoning ordinances prohibit such activities. Likewise, it is wrong to launch a new ministry without the resources unless there is a clear and unmistakable call of God to launch out completely as a faith ministry.

Tactical or Short-Term Planning

Tactical or short-term planning begins to develop the generalities of the strategic plan into specific action steps. This is accomplished by breaking the strategy down into intermediate steps and ultimately into daily activities. The old adage in business reminds us that the way to eat an elephant is one bite at a time. Tactical planning helps to carve up the overall plan into bite-sized chunks that can be actioned and accomplished incrementally. Nothing builds success like a little success. There is strong psychological power in giving that task a check mark and indicating that it is finished!

Tactical Planning

Starts with the Strategic Plan

Each element of the tactical plan must flow from the vision. Any ministry or activity that is not directly traceable back to the strategic plan is a rogue element detracting time and resources from the shared mission of the local church. Rogues and rabbit trails are the enemy of focus and will take you away from your goal and not toward it.

Strategies are the key element that links strategic and tactical planning models. Out of this linkage will flow how a strategic outcome will be accomplished, what new ministry will be started, how resources are allocated, and how success will be measured.

Successful Strategic Planning Primer

Every successful strategic plan will have some elements that are in common one with another. It is time to examine some of those common elements.

Deliberate Action Plan

Every successful strategic plan will have a deliberate action plan. Deliberate means that the plan has intentionality. There are specific and tangible aspects of the plan. Successful ministries know what they are about and why they exist. They are intentional. They are not accidental or haphazard. They have a set of steps and a path that they are walking that lead them to a well-defined destination. Leaders with intentionality get up every day knowing where they are going and knowing what they will do today to get them closer to the goal that Jesus Christ has given them.

Ownership of the Vision and Plan

Every successful strategic plan will have become the shared property of all who are encompassed by it and all who will implement it. No plan that is legislated upon the local church will succeed like one that is developed and adopted corporately. But, does this mean that everyone will see the vision, adopt the strategy and execute the plan on day one? Probably not. There is almost always a trickle down effect to vision and planning. Most often an organization will have a visionary leader somewhere on the team. And that person is often the first to catch the vision. But vision, like the flu, can be contagious if it is handled properly. Take the time up front to sell the plan and allow everyone to embrace the plan as though it were their own.

Vision and Values

Every successful strategic plan will have a well-defined and communicated vision for the task. This element contains the broadest possible description of the local church's vision for what God is calling it to do. This element may initially have a distinct philosophical tone. That tone must be refined and be made simple and fundamental.

An example of such a vision can be found in the "motto" of a local Church of the Nazarene in the suburban Washington, DC area. This vision statement was introduced fully one year before the leadership entered into the strategic planning process.

Their vision statement is "**Putting God First**" with the word "First" acting as an acrostic. That acrostic is as follows:

F ind your ministry
Every one should know their spiritual gift and be actively engaged in using it in the local church.
I nvest in the Kingdom
Every one in the local church is investing in the local church through tithes and offerings.
R each out in Redemption
Every one in the local church is reaching out with Christ's love and offering themselves as ministers of Jesus Christ to a lost and hurting world.
S ing to the Lord
Every one in the local church is an active participant in the corporate worship experience.

T EAM Evangelism
Every one in the local church is actively involved on some level in evangelistic activities through witnessing, hospitality or friendship.

By the time the leadership began introducing new plans and strategies to advance the cause of Christ in the local church, the congregation had already seen the communicated vision for the tasks that were to come. When the plans began to be introduced, the congregation could already see how they fit into the overall vision of the church.

External Needs Assessment
and Self-Evaluation

A successful strategic plan will have a good measure of reflection in the early stages. This time of reflection will look at both the external needs that the local church is facing and the strengths and weaknesses of the leadership to meet those needs. Every local church has strengths that they do not realize that they have. Even the small struggling church has strengths. Conversely, every church has weaknesses that they do not realize that they have. It is up to the leadership to discern and learn what to do in light of those strengths and weaknesses.

External Needs Assessment

This is an appraisal of the key outside forces that will influence the success that a local church may have in impacting its community. Surveys and demographic studies will provide the church with important information about the needs of the community. Interviewing other church leaders or civic leaders about the needs in the local area will also provide insight. This type of information gathering will cause you to realize that, although an elder day care center is a noble idea, it would be foolish for a church to undertake in a community of young single or newly married professionals.

Today, in the internet age, this information is readily available. It is also usually available for free if you are willing to scour the internet for demographic databases and resource material on your surrounding community.

Self-Evaluation

This is an appraisal of the key inside forces that will influence the success that a local church may have in impacting its community. Here is where the local church must use a facilitator to work with both pastoral staff and lay leaders to determine each leader's specific strengths and weaknesses. Ideally lay strengths will augment pastoral weaknesses. The opposite will also be true. It is important that this part be completed prior to any "planning". It is also important that this be completed in a spirit of mutual love and respect for one another.

The need for a facilitator cannot be overemphasized at this point. Select this individual carefully. I am partial to this person being a leading layman in either the local church or a neighboring church. This individual must have the skills of a facilitator. They must be able to be objective. They must be able to draw folks out and help them to open up and communicate their feelings, observations, and insights about themselves and the pastor. Having said this, the facilitator needs to be a "friendly and sympathetic" supporter of the pastor and the pastoral staff. This cannot degenerate into a clergy versus laity conversation.

Strategic Objectives

Strategic objectives are written statements that describe in detail the intended outcome. These statements include descriptions of the "target" or ministry focus. For something to be a strategic objective, it must have a specific timeframe for accomplishing the task. This, too, must be written. Strategic objectives do not need to have detailed plans associated with them at this point in the process. They can be best described from the 30,000 foot level.

Identifiable Mile Posts

Every successful strategic plan will however have a set of identifiable mile posts along the way. These mile posts will mark the journey and indicate to all if there is progress. Such passages will encourage everyone who is traveling on this journey. Passing significant mile posts are a cause to celebrate God's goodness and will also motivate the church to continue when the going gets tough.

Outcome Measures

An outcome measure is a yardstick, or standard, used to measure success in achieving a strategic objective. It measures how well the local church is doing. It indicates whether there is any impact upon the target.

Every strategic objective has an accompanying outcome measure. This outcome measure uses terms identical to the strategic objective that it measures. By comparing the quantity or quality in the outcome measure to the strategic objective's performance target, the church leadership can state clearly whether or not the church achieved its strategic objective.

Accurate Measurement Tools

Every successful strategic plan will have a set of accurate measurement tools or metrics. These tools will offer ample pointers toward the need for corrective action. Like mile posts, seeing your church performing well against an objective mark, these offer times of celebration for successes achieved and will be opportunities to offer our praise and thanks to God who provides the increase.

Effective Realignment Measures

Every successful strategic plan will have a set of effective realignment measures. It is a very rare thing to achieve complete success from the very outset without ever making any mistakes in planning and execution. These realignment measures serve to bring the project or venture back into line with the overall goals and objectives of the local church. This indicates the need for adaptability to changes in needs, resources or scope.

Strategic Priorities

Strategic priorities rank the strategic objectives according to their relative importance to the local church. This rank is determined by the vision and core values of the local church as well as the external needs assessment and the self-evaluation. These priorities are important to rank because they will set resource and budget decisions in the implementation phases.

Tactical Plans

Tactical plans are approaches or implementation methodologies. They are the concrete blueprints taken from the abstract or philosophical design sketches. These begin to answer the question, "How are we going to do it?"

In the tactical planning element, the leadership will identify all the alternate approaches, rate them according to the local churches needs and resources, and then select a set of tactical plans that will best achieve the strategic objective.

Performance Feed Forward

A performance feed forward is a systematic procedure for comparing actual performance against planned performance. This information is critically important to evaluating the recently completed plan and for subsequent planning cycles. This is different than performing the ongoing analysis and modification to an active plan. This is a deliberate program "post-mortem" or plan audit. If possible, this should be done by other than those who carried out the plan.

Tactical or Short-Term Planning

Self-Assessment

The process of tactical planning must include a step to determine the feasibility of the church to accomplish its stated vision. Please hear me when I say that this is not a litmus test for your faith. Rather, this is an assessment with the heart of a steward and with the sobering fact that the church is accountable for how the tithes and offerings are used in the building of God's Kingdom here on earth.

Tactical Objectives

Every element of the tactical plan must contain a set of short-range and intermediate goals that contribute to achieving the strategic plan. Franklin Quest has coined the term, SMART Goals. The word "SMART" serves as an excellent acrostic for basic goal setting techniques.

SMART Goals

S pecific — Each goal must address a specific need or objective.

M easurable — Each goal must have a way to evaluate success.

A ction Oriented — Each goal must be active and not passive.

R ealistic — Each goal must stretch your faith, but be realistic.

T imely — Each goal must have a specific timetable or deadline.

Output Measure

Output Measure

This aspect of tactical planning asks the question, "How do we know?" when we have reached our objectives.

If you don't know where you are, you can't tell how far you've come.

Resource Requirements

Tactical planning must consider what resources (time, money, personnel, etc.) it will take to accomplish the specific ministry objective.

Tactical Priorities

The most critical aspect of both tactical and strategic planning is determining our daily priorities and incorporating strategic action-oriented steps into our daily plans.

Why Plan?

Why should we bother to plan? Why not just trust God to provide the harvest. Here is an often misquoted and misunderstood portion of scripture.

> *And he said unto them, The harvest indeed is plenteous, but the laborers are few: pray ye therefore the Lord of the harvest, that he send forth laborers into his harvest.*
>
> Luke 10:2 ASV

Note that the prayer is not for the harvest. It is plenteous already! The harvest is the Lord's and He does not have lean harvests. The prayer is specifically for laborers to go and work in the harvest. Here is where planning is needed. First, a plan for getting laborers and, then, for organizing and working in the fields.

A pastor in one local church stated it best this way.

> *Where there is no vision or plan the people perish.*
>
> Proverbs. 29:18 - DWV (David Woods Version)

Or an anonymous philosopher said it this way.

> *"If you don't change your direction, you are likely to end up where you are going."*
>
> (Anon.)

One of my favorite sayings relative to this topic is this one.

> *"If you don't care where you are going, any road will get you there."*
>
> (Anon.)

Let's agree that planning, in and of itself, is not an unGodly activity. I know that for some who come from a very strong faith-based tradition, this will seem to be the case. But the Bible speaks to the need for planning. Luke 14:28 says;

> *"Suppose one of you wants to build a tower. Won't you first sit down and estimate the cost to see if you have enough money to complete it?"*

Clearly there is value in some advance thought and planning before beginning a significant activity. This verse speaks to a building project. This is something that many churches know a great deal about. But the principles in the verse speak to the value of planning and the importance of a well thought out approach to developing and executing projects, programs and ministries in the local church.

How do we plan?

How Do We Plan?

How do we Plan? The fact is that many of us do not! And therein lies the problem. It seems that part of our culture here in the United States is that we like to "fly by the seat of the pants" and we value the impromptu or spontaneous nature of many of our personalities. So, consider the following quick facts and figures.

Interesting Tidbits on Planning

A recent survey by a major time management company revealed the following data.

Daily Planning

32% never plan their daily work
45% plan only once a week
23% plan only occasionally
Only 9% accomplish what they plan

Working Toward Goals

37% frequently work on what they say they want to accomplish
33% seldom or never work toward a specific goal
30% occasionally work toward a goal

Planning Tools

52% use a "month-at-a-glance" style calendar
29% use organizers or "planners" such as the Day-Timer, Day Runner or Franklin Planner.
19% use napkins, envelops, sticky notes, etc.

Daily Ministry Process

Every day we must pray and ask ourselves three questions:
>   Why are we doing this?
>   Where are we going?
>   What are we doing to get there?

Today we have the distinct opportunity to succeed or fail as the leadership of the church. Taking ownership of these concepts allows us to accomplish anything the Lord empowers and directs.

The Battle of Cowpens

The Battle of Cowpens, North Carolina

Let's take a final look at the issue of strategic planning. The following is a clear example of having a plan and then executing that plan successfully. Once again, it is a military illustration from Pastor David Woods.

General Daniel Morgan, under the command of General Nathaniel Greene, was charged with protecting North Carolina from an invading force of British Regulars during the Revolutionary War. The British Regulars were under the command of General George Cornwallis.

Gen. Morgan had only a force of 750 troops, and only about 180 of those were Continental soldiers. The rest were comprised of freshly recruited, local militiamen. These were to make a stand against a 1,000 man force of highly trained British Regulars.

Gen. Morgan chose a small hill to make his stand upon and there developed one of the most brilliantly conceived and executed tactical plans in world military history. He divided his militia into two parallel lines in front of the hill. He placed the more highly trained Continentals up on the hilltop.

He instructed the first line of the militiamen to fire upon the advancing British and then quickly fall back behind the second line. Once the British approached the second line, they too would fire and then fall back behind the hill. They did exactly as planned and instructed. As they fell back, the British interpreted it as a rout and rushed headlong into the guns of the waiting Continental soldiers.

As the British battled the Continentals, a small force of cavalry that was held in reserve by Gen. Morgan, rushed from behind the hill and hit the British flank hard and by surprise. Simultaneously, the regrouped militiamen now rushed out from behind the hill and hit the opposite flank. This is a classic military maneuver known as a "Double Envelopment."

The British were soundly defeated in a critical prelude to their ultimate defeat and unconditional surrender at Yorktown, Virginia. This was a crucial turning point in America's fight for independence.

The lesson from this is simple and obvious. "Planning works!" It works in military campaigns, in business enterprises, and it works in ministry in the local church. Don't be afraid to plan. It is not an indicator of your lack of faith. Instead, it is a recognition that God has granted us a measure of intelligence and strength and He expects us to develop and utilize them in carrying out the ministry that He has given us.

There are many who would say upon reading these concepts that planning is an indicator of our lack of faith. I would submit to you that it takes very little faith to seek a vision for what God wants us to do. There is no personal cost to see a vision. Real faith is exercised the moment that we accept the calling that we feel is from God. And it is at that point that even the function of planning is an act of faith because we may not even see the resources at hand that we will need to accomplish the mission to which we are called.

Planning Pitfalls and Guarantees for Failure

Surely there are dangers lurking for the unsuspecting strategic planner. The following lists are taken from the business and commercial setting. Nevertheless, they transfer extremely well to the subject at hand. Some of them also contain a little humor. Some are subtle, some are not so subtle.

Top 10 Planning Pitfalls

1. The "We-do that already" Mentality
2. A "Not-invented-here" Attitude
3. Stakeholder Suppression (nobody needs to know what I'm doing)
4. Short-Term Incentive Plan
5. Lack of Creativity (Lack of Ability)
6. The "We Don't Have time (to do things right)" Excuse
7. Tunnel Vision and the Financial Bean Counters
8. The "We Don't Speak to Each Other" Excuse
9. Corporate Culture Paralysis
10. Incorrect Identification of the Businesses - (Fruit Salad Syndrome)

10 Ways to Guarantee Failure

1. Assume planning is not important to the success of the business.
2. Do not plan with other departments.
3. Do not communicate a shared vision.
4. Use last year's never-supported plan with a few minor changes.

5. Mail a big package of forms to department heads.
6. Buy Porter's books and automatically assume you're an expert planner.
7. Write "competitive advantage" three times fast and assume you have it.
8. Use a short-term and narrow reward system.
9. Be in competition with other departments rather than cooperate with them.
10. Don't think; and never be creative.

Ten More Ways to Guarantee Failure

1. Do not link strategy with implementation.
2. Avoid measurement systems which gauge success.
3. Expand the size of the planning department to indicate how important it is.
4. Be quick to blame the person next to you.
5. Fire people often to show Wall Street analysts you can make tough decisions.
6. Focus on internal transfer pricing issues every Tuesday and Thursday.
7. Spend most of your time looking at the numbers - any numbers.
8. Never re-allocate or retrain staff; only fire and hire and fire again.
9. Blame poor results on the sales force and/or the customer.
10. Do not hold anyone accountable for the planning process.

Self-Evaluations and Reviews

This section is included mostly as an example of the kinds of discussion topics used in one of the churches that I worked with to implement the *MFV2A* process and methodology. It indicates some of the specifics that resulted from a self-evaluation of the lay leadership in that local church and a pastoral review. The self-evaluation was conducted via a questionnaire and some personal interviews, while the pastoral review was conducted via a questionnaire developed by and for the pastor.

The lay leaders were asked to look at their own leadership position and consider what were their strengths and weaknesses. And the pastor was asked to take a look with a similar lens.

Many who read this section will recognize this process as being similar to a "SWOT" analysis that is utilized in the secular and commercial marketplace.

SWOT is a structured planning method used to evaluate the strengths, weaknesses, opportunities, and threats involved in a project or in a business venture. A SWOT analysis can be carried out for a product, place, industry or person. It involves specifying the objective of the business venture or project and identifying the internal and external factors that are favorable and unfavorable to achieve that objective.

Clearly this is a business tool. But the concept and the analysis is sound and applicable to the church world as well.

Revisiting the Self-Evaluation

Revisiting the Lay Leadership Self-Evaluation

What can we say about lay leadership?

Typical Areas of Strength:
Empowerment - Released to do something with the authority to do it.
Broad leadership base - Team Structure
Open to ideas and discussion
Spirit of unity, cooperation and dedication
Adaptability - somewhat. Not ready to completely change structure of worship, etc.
Dealing with vision and ministry items - Beginning to create time for discussion. Still need communication with rest of congregation.

Typical Areas for Improvement:
Communication - use report flow. This is mainly for internal communication.
Follow through - accountability. How do we know if we are following through, and who is responsible for guaranteeing the follow-through? Example: Roof repair - many were checking with the Sunday School Superintendent from time to time. The individual accepting the assignment is responsible for guaranteeing follow-through and communicating action/results.
Working between meetings (balance.) What are we doing to accomplish what we have been charged to do?

Central direction or focus - Need to understand what is our foundation, our dearest value. Out of that will come the focus.

Boldness and a prayer focus - Re-establish Prayer Chain

Faithful support of church activities

Revisiting the Pastoral Review

Revisiting the Pastoral Review

What can we say about Pastoral Leadership?

Typical Areas of Strength:
Spirit of cooperation - assimilation of other ideas, closely working with ministry team leaders
Preaching and teaching skills
Planning and vision skills - Broad based
Resourcefulness and creative thinking - varies structure of services for interest and impact, Focus on the Family videos Wed. nights
Shepherding
Sensitive to the people
Music and Worship
Compassion (shows emotion)
Leadership
Patience
Sensitive to the Spirit
Commitment and Accountability

A good discussion needs to take place regarding the involvement of lay persons in areas of worship leadership. It is easier to be asked to do something than to volunteer to do it. It has been observed that we all have an 80% perfection level, and will do the job ourselves if we don't think someone else can do it at 80% level. The problem seems to stem from the point of view that the EGO is involved when we volunteer to sing a special, read the Scripture, etc., regardless of our desires to be involved. The question is how to communicate this desire to the leadership. Leadership needs to become more involved in the daily lives of the membership to be able to discern some of these desires, and to utilize them.

Typical Areas for Improvement

Too clock conscious - worries about ending the service in a timely manner, when he should be totally sensitive to not quenching the Spirit

"Prays around the world"

Does too much by himself (one man show)

Could listen more...talk less in counseling settings

Allow more time for acceptance of new ideas - Older members of the congregation need more time to accept change

Increase communication - Sometimes the idea has been "out there", but not communicated adequately. Need better ways to get ideas accepted.

Intolerant of distractions in pursuit of an objective - (actually it can be a strength as well)

Reacts quickly to criticism - somewhat tied to the perceived intolerance of distractions

Areas of Particular Significance

Areas of Particular Significance

What areas of concern deserve our priority attention?

Significant Strengths (Sample)
> Dealing with vision and ministry items - Coming away with value system in place, knowing what is important.
> Broad leadership base - varied levels of expertise.
> Resourcefulness and creative thinking - i.e. Missions emphases on Sunday nights, building a sense of competition in the Sunday School with "Donut Olympics", etc.
> Worshipping together - Excellent spirit in all services, good congregational singing, etc.
> Spirit of Openness and Unity, with right attitudes.

Significant Improvement Areas (Sample)
> Delegation – Releasing control and giving more authority to others.
> Communication – Dialog at "piddly" level to get to significant levels.
> Accountability – At the same level as delegation, accepting responsibility and delegating responsibility. Also need to be more intent and careful in how we ask for accountability, in loving concern, not in confrontation and judgment.
> Central Direction or focus – Keeping "the main thing the main thing."

Balance - Being able to redeem time to do what is most important to us (Moving from maintenance to ministry.)

What is the "Franklin Model"

What is the "Franklin Model"?

The Franklin Planner, is a paper-based time management system created by Hyrum W. Smith and known as FranklinQuest prior to an acquisition in 1997 by the Stephen R. Covey's Covey Leadership Center. The Franklin Day Planner was first produced in 1984. There followed a time-management workshop, which emphasized clarification of personal values, priorities and mission. Taken as a whole, it is known by many as the *Franklin Model*.

It consists physically of a ring binder holding specially designed loose-leaf pages. It is divided by monthly tabs between the pages and accepts a wide variety of specialized accessories and inserts to customize each binder to best benefit the owner. The system aims to consolidate tasks and appointments along with personal records in one place for improved personal information management by eliminating "floating pieces of paper".

Smith named his planning system after Benjamin Franklin (1706-1790), who famously kept a small private book as detailed in his autobiography.

A core technique of the Franklin Planner system involves beginning each day with fifteen minutes of "solitude and planning". I have expanded this time and added a time of Bible reading and devotion on the front end of the solitude and planning time.

Because of its overall design, the Franklin-Covey system lends itself to be used as a massive and systematic "tickler file", as well as a long-range planner. Most annual versions of the page inserts for the Franklin system include yearly calendars for at least five years; future monthly calendars for at least three years; and then the current year's pages and associated monthly calendars for planning. When used as a total package, the system provides a means of tracking minute details; storage of signed agreements (especially if pages are archived in the archival binders); and tracking of business and personal expenses for taxes.

Working the "Franklin Model"

Working The "Franklin Model" - Part 1

What is the "Franklin Model"?
- A productivity pyramid
- Governing Values - determining at the lowest possible level what drives us
- Long Range Goals - What do I finally want to accomplish?
- Intermediate Steps - What are some major milestones along the way?
- Daily Tasks - Action items that help me accomplish my goals
- Bringing daily activities in line with governing values - being sure you are doing the things that will accomplish the goals
- Core values drive the planning process - Must discover and identify these values before we can build on them. What is our foundation?

Everyone has a unique set of values, though most Christians have similar foundational values. Sometimes there is a disparity between what we claim is our core value and our daily activities. It is easy to get caught up in the daily routine and neglect our basic goals.

Based on what we discussed this morning: What are some core values for this local Church?
- Concern for the lost - evangelizing our community
- Concern for individual family's spiritual condition

- Sensitivity to the Spirit - We are sensitive to the Holy Spirit in our daily lives. This is demonstrated by:
- Concern for the lost
- Our love and acceptance of people
- Spending time in daily devotion
- Spirit-led use of our time
- Long -Range Goals - providing a map to being you in line with core value:
- Doing something new
- Time based - Date set for accomplishment
- Develop long range goal - save enough money for vacation; will build a new home next year; will lose 50 pounds by the end of 2014.

Value: Sensitivity to the Needs of the Community

LONG RANGE GOAL: Elder Care Program by 2000 (Sample)

This Elder Care will house senior citizens during working hours. This releases adult children to continue their employment.

Intermediate Steps

- Milestones on the journey - checkpoints
- Specific Tasks - "Stuff" that happens that I can definitely relate to
- Develop Intermediate Steps
- Survey Community for need by May 1997
- Space Analysis of current facility by May 1997
- Funding determined by facility/survey
- Licensing - Apply by January 1998

Daily Tasks

- Where the rubber meets the road
- What can I do today that will take me in the direction I have decided is important for me to go?
- Develop daily tasks

Summary

- What is the underlying foundation?
- What long-range goals have I set?
- What mile markers will I pass along the way?
- What tasks will translate that into action?

Resources

- Franklin Planner
- Ascend and Values Quest (Software Program)
- Seminars

Franklin Planner Inserts are given to each participant at this point. The seminar leader will describe how to organize the binders, beginning with current month, etc.

Keep three months in planner at all times -- Last month, current month, next month.

Rules

1. You now have one, and only one, calendar
2. Keep planner with you at all times
3. Eliminate all loose paper

Updated for 2014

There has been incredible growth and development in the area of personal organizational tools since the first edition of this was published in 1996. One of the tools that has become more than just a simple email and calendar tool is the set of tools and the functionality built into Microsoft's Outlook. Outlook has become the "gold standard" for email, calendaring and task management in many corporations and non-profit organizations.

Notwithstanding, there are specific tools that are available today that take personal organization and effectiveness to a level not thought possible with Franklin Planners and the integration with Steven Covey's work back in the late 1990s. I am particularly intrigued by Evernote. I have recently adopted it as my "digital brain" and I use it exclusively for managing all of the bits and pieces of information that I collect throughout the day. I have also begun using Nozbe for task management. These two tools (both of which have totally free versions that you can use) have revolutionized my organizational effectiveness as much as the Franklin Planner did for me in the 1990s.

For more information on using these tools, consult their individual websites. I would also point you to Michael Hyatt's website for the methodology and system that I copied from him. He has some great articles on his website that speak to his evolution with Evernote. Here is a great place to start to learn about how to use Evernote. http://michaelhyatt.com/a-handy-index-to-all-my-evernote-posts.html And here is a link regarding Nozbe. http://michaelhyatt.com/tag/nozbe

Really Working the "Franklin Model"

Really Working "Franklin Model" -- Part 2
(Sample to write on today's page)
- Values
- Committed to Outreach (*See below Core Value sample*)
- Committed to Relationships
- Committed to Communications
- Committed to Accountability
- Committed to Worship
- Committed to Putting God First

On second Specialty Tab - Goal Planning - Values

CORE VALUE: Committed to Outreach (*Sample from above*)

Attributes of Value:

Caring for others; follow-up; assimilation; entrance point seminars; open and comfortable setting; friendly; relationships

Clarifying Statement:

We will offer redemption and reflect an attitude of openness, compassion and sincerity by developing relationships and ministries to meet needs. We will provide an open and comfortable setting with multiple entrance points, and work toward assimilating people and gifts into the body by demonstrating Christ's love.

LONG RANGE GOALS (Sample)

Follow-up Tool by January 2014

Develop a proven follow-up tool to track guests and prospects

25% community presence in the church by February 2014

The community is within a 5-mile radius

Sponsor 3 Needs-Based Community Events in 2014

AA Chapter meetings
Financial seminars
Grief Recovery
Single Parenting
Divorce Recovery

INTERMEDIATE STEPS (Sample)

GOAL - Follow-up Tool

- Evangelism & Outreach Team to Identify and recommend tool to Church Board at the November meeting
- Inform, educate, and implement tool by January 2014

DAILY ACTIVITIES (Sample)

Goal #1

Dave Woods to call Larry Burns - Team leader
Set meeting with Pastor, Dave, Larry
Gather current tools

Team prepares recommendation
Present E/O recommendation

Goal #2
Call _____
Write _____
Attend a training session
Demonstrate your plan in action

Closing Thoughts

At the end of the day, this is about leadership. It is about the leadership of the Holy Spirit in our lives and whether or not we will follow. And it is about our leadership skills and abilities as demonstrated in the local church.

I commend you and the rest of the church leadership for reading this resource material and for at least considering doing something to move from vision to action. Let's be honest after reading this little book, the church is pretty good at seeing the vision of what God is calling us to do. The very word "vision" sounds supernatural. But many of us just don't know how to translate that vision into action.

Part of the problem sometimes is that we either get scared so by the vision that we do nothing in response. Or, we get so excited that we run ahead of God and mess everything up. I believe that the very God that gave you the vision will provide the tactical guidance that you will need. And maybe, just maybe, He wants to use this resource and these principles to help you. Do you think that is possible?

Let us agree to commit to what God has called us to, and let us also commit to agree that we will work together as God leads.

You can find more leadership issues and inspiration at
http://leadershipvoices.com
You can also reach out to the author via email at
kevin@leadershipvoices.com
You can follow him on Twitter at @LeadershipIs
And you can become a fan on their Facebook page at
http://www.facebook.com/LeadershipVoicesLLC

www.ingramcontent.com/pod-product-compliance
Lightning Source LLC
Chambersburg PA
CBHW020522030426

42337CB00011B/516